Lending a Hand

By Cameron Macintosh

It can be fun to lend a hand.

We can do lots of things
to help.

Criss mends things
to lend a hand.

Nell comes and runs
with Pop's dog!

You can lend a hand
to Mum and Dad.

Steff lends a hand by
picking things up at home.

Sandy tends the pond
for Mum and Dad.

Rand picks up trash
on the sand.

And Tess picks up trash
on the land!

You can lend a hand
when Gran is sick.

You can hand her a gift.

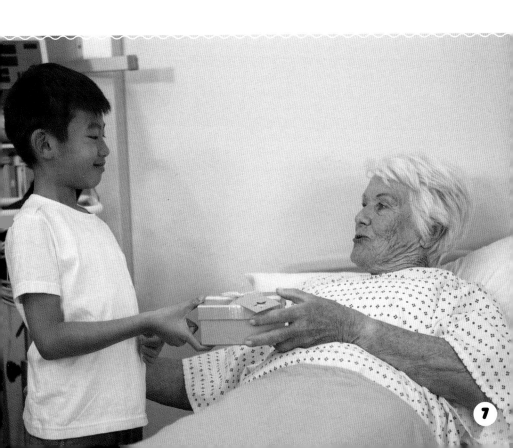

We can do lots of
little things to lend a hand.

You can just stand
and have a good long chat.

What will you do to lend a hand?

CHECKING FOR MEANING

1. How does Steff lend a hand at home? *(Literal)*

2. Who helps Mum and Dad care for the pond? *(Literal)*

3. How do you feel when you have helped at home? *(Inferential)*

EXTENDING VOCABULARY

mends	What does *mends* mean in this text? What things do you have that sometimes need to be mended? What are other words with a similar meaning? E.g. fixed, repaired.
picking	Look at the word *picking*. What is the base word? Now look at the word *lending* on the front cover. Can you find the base word in the text?
tends	What does this word mean? Can you think of other words that mean the same? E.g. cares for, looks after.

MOVING BEYOND THE TEXT

1. How can you lend a hand at school? What are some jobs you could do in the classroom? In the playground?

2. Why is it important to lend a hand sometimes?

3. Can you think of a time when someone helped you? What did you say to them? How did you feel?

4. Do you ever lend a hand without being asked? Why?

SPEED SOUNDS

ft	mp	nd	nk	st

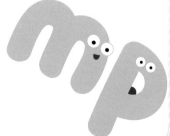

PRACTICE WORDS

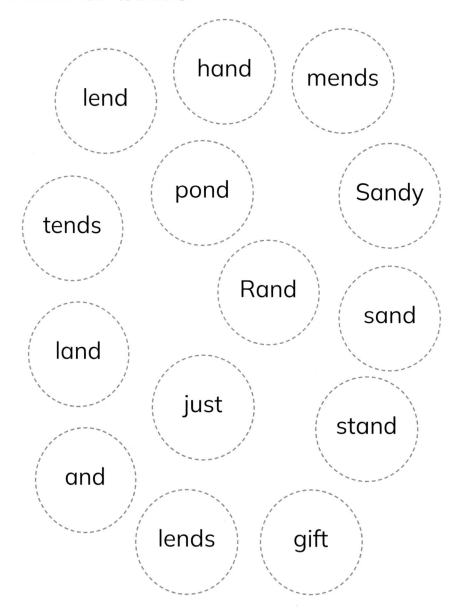

lend

hand

mends

pond

Sandy

tends

Rand

sand

land

just

stand

and

lends

gift